THE

MOMMS

MOUNTAINEERING CHALLENGE

AN

ESSENTIAL

MULTI GUIDE

TO HELP YOU COMPLETE

THE

ECCENTRICAL FEATS OF THE MOMMS POEM

BY

TREVOR ATKINSON

TREVOR ATKINSON

Born 1955 in Wakefield West Yorkshire a family man with a passion for adventure, exploration and mountaineering. A climber of the Matterhorn, Monte Rosa Dufourspitze (the highest mountain in Switzerland) with seven ascents of Mont Blanc (the highest peak in the west of modern Europe) and with numerous other ascents in the Alps.

He once camped at 18,000 feet under the shadows of Mount Everest on the Sola Khumbu reaching a personal high point of 19,500 feet. He has also climbed Africa's snow capped highest peak Uhuru on Kilimanjaro at 19,340 feet. A well travelled mountaineer whose experiences range from the Icelandic Vatnajökull to the Snowy mountains of Australia, from the jungle volcanoes of Bali to bivouacking on the desert summit of Mount Sinai.

He spent 12 years voluntary service in a Moorland Rescue Team based on the Yorkshire Pennines and raced in marathons including Snowdonia, London, Dublin, Paris and New York, he also took part in the Ben Nevis Fell race finishing 2nd (from last) and officially last in the 1996 Scottish Coast to Coast cycle, run and canoe endurance race with a time of 20 hours 59 minutes 22 seconds ....BUT FINISHED.

Dedicated to Amy,
and the memory of Grandad Jack.

ISBN 1-903568-02-1

First Published 2002

CHALLENGE PUBLICATIONS

CONTENTS:

Page

ILLUSTRATIONS:

MOMMS TIPS:

PHOTOGRAPHS:

Acknowledgements

A special thank you to all my colleagues and genuine mountaineering friends for unselfishly helping to make this book a reality.

Berwyn Williams for his support and supplying photographs.

Brian G Smailes of Challenge Publication for help and friendly advice.

Brian Smith and Iolo Jones for checking technical details.

Bethesda Mountaineering Club.

Front Cover Photograph Malcolm Davis

Diane Sharpe for advise and encouragement.

Janet Atkinson for general support and tireless proof reading.

DISCLAIMER

Neither author nor publisher can accept any responsibility for accidents or injury sustained in the course of this Momms challenge. As with any other potentially dangerous sport climbers and mountaineers alike are reminded that safety and appropriate mountain skills are the responsibility of the participating individuals and the challenge book merely guides you through the Momms poem.

The information recorded in this book is believed by the author to be correct at publication. No liabilities can be accepted for any inaccuracies which may be found. It is recommended that anyone using this book should refer to the relevant map in conjunction with the book and be experienced in map recognition and compass use.
The description or representation of a route used does not necessarily mean there is existence of a right of way.

INTRODUCTION

"There comes a time to take a chance
With skill and nerve and high romance."

MOUNTAINEERS OF METTLE
&
MOUNTAIN SOCIETY

THE MOMMS

As a child, I'd read a novel about a fantasy adventure based on two children being chased around an area of countryside near Alderley Edge in Cheshire by goblins, witches and other strange creatures. With the help of a wizard, some dwarfs and friendly elfs they survived to reach a prominent grassy peak known as Shutlingsloe above Macclesfield forest where on its slopes the story line came to a climatic and very dramatic conclusion.

Now to this day you can visit and follow the very story line of that book by being there and witnessing in your own imagination where it happened. It was this interacting with fiction that gave me the initial idea to interact with a poem. Not just any poem, but a poem made up of multi challenges, feats and mountaineering skill, for we mountaineers a challenge laid down is like a red flag to a bull, an adventure a mission, to see a mountain is to climb it, why! "Because it's there", of course! - was Mallory's response.

The much sought after Momms badge depicts 12 of the main feats *(Fig No 1, page 33)* of the mountaineering challenge with the exception of the Snowdon Horseshoe and Jack's Rake on Pavey Ark. At intervals in the book I've put together some relevant Momms guidance reminders on mountain skills and first aid called *Momms tips.*

We Mom we climb to show our Mettle
feat not achieved thou need not settle.

THE CHALLENGE

The Momms mountaineering feats are based on all round mountaineering ability, fitness, endurance and nerve. You don't have to be an expert but it helps to be a confident all round mountaineer with a strong sense of adventure.

We start with the ascent of Shutlingsloe in the Cheshire hills where the Momms idea was born, then we follow our feats of adventure with the ascents of Ben Nevis, Snowdon and Scafell Pike, the Yorkshire three peaks walk with ascents of Pen y ghent, Whernside and Ingleborough. A 12.000 feet or above ascent of an Alpine peak or the equivalent in height of any mountain of your choice and at least one crossing of the classic Welsh XIV 3000 mountain challenge completed within 24 hours.

Jack's Rake a rocky scramble on the exposed face on Pavey Ark at Langdale in the Lake District, the north ridge of Tryfan scramble with the leap of faith from Adam to Eve summit rocks for the freedom of the mountain followed by an exposed scramble up onto Bristly Ridge an exposed exhilarating pinnacle rock scramble (not footpath).

The Snowdon Horseshoe of Crib Goch, Crib y Ddysgl, Snowdon and Y Lliwedd, a 300 feet rock climb on a graded route of your choice to prove technical ability either leader or second with rope in use with a full understanding of belays and abseiling. Climb and cross the Castell y Gwynt, "Castle of the winds," on the Glyderau range, then finally scramble up the Braich ty du Pinnacle on Pen yr Ole Wen's Pinnacle ridge, this is washed down with a celebratory pint in the Victoria Hotel in Bethesda followed by any other pub that can be found in this friendly and hard working Welsh town.

So read the poem carefully and tick off the list near the back of the book, just follow the page-by-page guide along with mountaineering tips and don't forget the curse in the last verse.

SHUTLINGSLOE 1659ft

Hidden away in Cheshire to the south east of Macclesfield, above the Macclesfield forest stands the prominent grassy peak of Shutlingsloe, known locally as the Cheshire Matterhorn a peak surrounded with magical aurora, legends and myth.

A mystical place where countless children's imaginations have witnessed the strange illustrative creatures to have crossed it's summit and slopes, a place of wizards, goblins and elves. This is our starting point of adventure and quest, the start of the Momms Mountaineering challenge, the peak from where the idea was nurtured lies here.

In the heart of Macclesfield forest next to the Trentabank reservoir G.R. 964711 (OS Landranger No 118) you will find the Ranger Information Centre with car park and Public Toilets. From the car park turn right onto the tarmac road, within 100 yards you will find a large double gate with a notice board nearby, keep on the tarmac road for another 100 yards and you will see on your right a signpost "Wildboarclough via Shutingsloe." Small steps lead up to a kissing gate and another signpost pointing the way up the steep forest bank.

Carry straight on up the path until it merges with a larger track joining from the right, again the track steepens as you push on up the side of Nessits Hill with a steep slope dropping down through the forest on your left, the track levels off before a final steep rise until a kissing gate is reached, ignoring the path on the right, carry straight on until you leave the shade of the forest pines, a signpost prompts you to the right passing the memorial bench and you emerge from the forest at a kissing gate onto a paved path that leads across the moorland until your first views of Shutlingsloe's pointed grassy peak.

Cross the moor to the wooden ramp that meets the stile and turn right following the wall to a stone stepped stile below the rocky summit, not the hardest ascents by all means but enough to make you pause for breath as you climb up it's rather steep rocky side on a series of stone steps. It's summit views stretch out across the Cheshire plains to the Radio Telescope at Jodrel Bank, while in the east the White Peak area of Derbyshire blossoms on the near horizon, so sit, study and take stock for this is where your Momms Challenge starts, "good luck and take care."

SHUTLINGSLOE 1659 ft

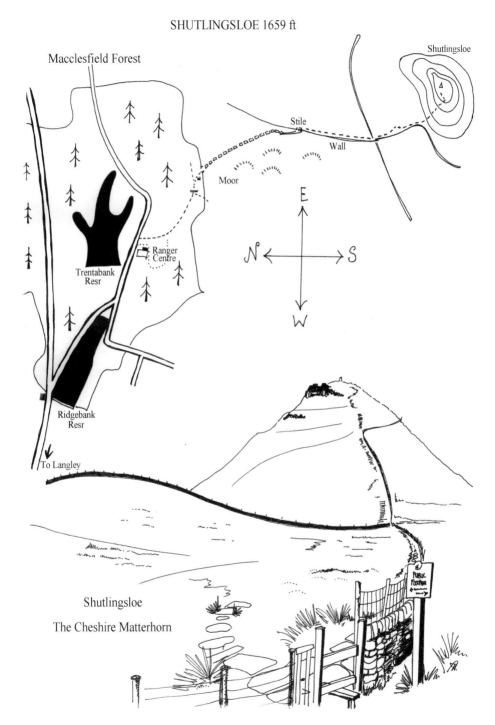

Shutlingsloe

Macclesfield Forest

Shutlingsloe

Stile

Wall

Moor

Ranger
Centre

Trentabank
Resr

E

N ← → S

W

Ridgebank
Resr

To Langley

Shutlingsloe

The Cheshire Matterhorn

PUBLIC
FOOTPATH

"To earn the badge just come along
endure the challenge of the Mom,
Ben Nevis to climb and conquer"

BEN NEVIS

Ben Nevis is the highest peak in the British Isles and stands at 4.406 feet above sea level.

It's huge north east face towers some 2.000 feet high in places and stretches two miles in length, it's north facing gullies carry remnants of the winter snow for most of the summer, snow patches can be found on the lower summit plateau until May and June.

Any would be Mom worth his, or her, salt should know that Ben Nevis is situated slightly south east of Fort William in a mountain district know as Lochaber in the highlands of Scotland, if you take the A 82 (T) Inverness road out of Fort William heading for Spean Bridge within a quarter of a mile, at the Nevis bridge roundabout, take the road signposted for Glen Nevis and follow this with the river Nevis on your left-hand side.

Within two mile, you'll have passed the main Glen Nevis caravan - campsite on your right, and then at the youth hostel the telephone box marks the starting point. Across the road, there's a wooden platform bridge crossing the river, the path feeds across this where you pass a large signpost displaying a description of Ben Nevis and current information on the weather forecast etc.

Climb up the steep stony rugged path until you meet the main tourist route and follow the main path up, slowly turning the lower ramparts of the Meall an Suidhe.

At 500 metres a conservation area reroutes the path to the left and then brings you out next to a small lock, expect it to be wet under foot here for it's a natural drainage area.

Map Fig No 2

BEN NEVIS

4.406 ft Summit

GLEN NEVIS

Carn Mor Dearg

Carn Dearg

Arete

C.I.C. Hut

Loch

Red Burn waterfall

Tourist Route

River Nevis

campsite

Bridge

Telephone

Achintee

To Fort William

Allt a Mhuilinn

Summit

Arete

Carn Mor Dearg

C.I.C Hut

Red Burn

Achintee

Bridge

Telephone Box

Campsite

S

E

W

N

7

Move over wet ground slowly rising to a major T- junction, turn right here onto undulating ground until you reach the waterfall at Red Burn (a good place for lunch and rest).

If you turn left at the T - junction the path feeds you up and over into the Allta Mhuilinn under the great crags of the north-east face and up to the CIC hut (Charles Inglis Clark hut).

From the CIC hut it's possible to gain the ridge of Carn Mor Dearg and it's summit at 3.475 feet (summer only) and cross the Carn Mor Dearg Arete a spectacular ridge scramble, climbing Ben Nevis from the south-east then descend via the tourist route.

Having rested at Red Burn, continue following the large foot path onto the zigzag section and snake your way up the endless grind until the lower summit plateau is reached, this is where you'll usually find snow on the lower ramparts of the summit plateau as it levels off onto the summit boulder field.

Beware of gullies on your left hand side (this is the north face) and keep off any snow or cornice edges you may find in these gullies, they are extremely treacherous. Follow the path onto the summit where a large cairn balances the trig point, to the right on a mound of rocks lies an emergency shelter next to the ruins of the observatory 1883 to 1904 and next to this is the highest war memorial in Britain.

Even in summer you can find the cold wind penetrating the body so after a reasonable rest and a bite to eat retrace your steps and descend down the path, you'll soon warm up, (don't forget to drink regularly or dehydration will set in).

To descend in bad weather a compass grid bearing of 231 from the summit for 150 metres, then follow grid bearing of 281 this will take you clear of the plateau and onto the main path. *(See Fig No 2)*

SNOWDON YR WYDDFA

VIA THE PYG TRACK:

Snowdon the highest mountain in England and Wales at 3.560 feet above sea level stands proud over the Snowdonia National Park. There are numerous paths leading to it's demanding and popular summit, even a rack and pinion railway snakes it's way up from Llanberis to the summit cafe that stands perched over looking Snowdon's western slopes of Cwm Clogwyn.

The Pyg track, a quick and popular route up Snowdon, with a three mile walk and 2.400 feet of ascent should take the average climber / walker about 2 to 3 hours, with a possible two hour descent.

Start from the car park at Pen y Pass (it's very busy at bank holidays and there's a charge for parking). In the upper right corner of the car park, through the gap in the wall, the path begins.

A rocky flagged path that steps it's way steeply at first up through large boulders. The obvious undulating path worms it's way up, the imposing peak of Crib Goch defends the near horizon dominating the views ahead.

Eventually Bwlch Moch pass is gained (Pass of the pigs) and the path levels out, the ramparts of the Crib Goch ridge are now visible ahead high on the right and spectacular views to the left of the mountain lake of Llyn Llydaw with the mountain face of Lliwedd dominating it's side of the valley.

The obvious path levels off and carries straight on south-westerly running the gauntlet of the southern slopes of Crib Goch, the path continues until views of the higher cwm are gained.

Running parallel with the path down on the left the deep blue waters of Glaslyn lay protected by the soaring trinities of the Snowdon face that are towering above it.

Care should be taken here in wet conditions, watch out for the marker cairns and continue up, crossing scree and loose rocks, until the man made staircase is gained.

SNOWDON

The path then zigzags it's way upwards towards a monolithic column that guards the ridge (from here beware of trains and high winds) turn left and an uncomplicated path leads you directly upwards to the summit running parallel with the high cliffs on the left hand side and the railway on your right.

As you approach the final section, you'll see the cafe building down to your right and at last the great dry stone mound holding the summit trig is gained and if you are lucky, Snowdon is briefly all yours.

In bad weather follow the directions of the railway to the monolith rock turn right and you are on the Pyg track.

The Pyg track as seen from the summit of Snowdon.

These we climb with passion
on Scafell Pike summit we aim to meet.

SCAFELL PIKE

In the south-west corner of the English Lake District at the northern tip of Wastwater lies an area know as Wasdale Head, a magical place totally surrounded by mountains except for the three mile long lake of deep blue bottomless water that cradles in the soaring scree ramparts of the Scafell satellites.

Scafell Pike the highest mountain in England, standing at 3,210 feet above sea level. There are various ways of reaching the summit, but via Mickledore the route is strenuously quick and magnificent taking two hours hard slog with an ascent of 3.000 feet.

The tourist route from Wasdale Head branches off at Hollow Stones and follows a more passive well cairned route up via Lingmel Col passing between Pikes Crag on the right and Dropping Crag on the left, this makes a good descent route in bad weather.

Drive to the northern tip of Wastwater where a narrow right hand turn down over a stone bridge brings you to a tree covered car park next to a campsite (the parking is free). G.R.183074. The ascent of Scafell Pike starts here.

Out of the car park to the left, follow the lane directly over a wooden bridge. There's a track on the left, follow this to the left of the Brackenclose climbers hut, walk up through the trees keeping Lingmell Gill on your left, a small wooden bridge is reached, cross this and move upwards to your right passing through the kissing gate.

The stony narrow path feeds you steeply up through bracken and trees to the sound of the cascading stream until another gate is reached, a very pronounced cobble path feeds you to the bottom of Brown Tongue where two main streams feed into a boulder strewn basin.

Looking back from the summit plateau of Scafell Pike towards Scafell and
Mickledore Pass, the route feeds in from the right hand side of the pass below
the dark crags of the upper cwm.

Cross the stream, hopefully keeping boots and feet dry, here the newly built stone staircase path soars steeply up the right hand side of the Brown Tongue, "heads down and sweat it out at this stage." Up hill the path gradually levels out a little at Hollow Stones, a large cairn marks the place where the path splits up when almost level with Black Crag on your right hand side. This deviation takes you directly up to Mickledore.

To the left of the cairn the tourist route leads up a more grassy, gentler route following the cairns up via Lingmell Col.

Now to Mickledore! A more direct route up into the boulder strewn upper Cwm below the tremendous crags of Scafell on your right, a large gigantic boulder marks the way, keep to the left of the upper Cwm following a steep shaly path up the screes, until a small wet gully is reached.

An easy scramble brings you onto the Mickledore Pass where a Mountain Rescue stretcher box can be found on the left. Follow the path left passing the stretcher box, then steeply up onto the lower boulder field where well spaced cairns feed you upwards, moving higher over awkward rugged rocks. The route feeds round in a half circle to the left at first and then to the right until the main tourist route from Lingmell Col is reached.

A sharp rocky rise brings you onto the barren wilderness of the rough desolate summit plateau of the highest mountain in England 3.210 feet. A large man-made circular cairn is found on the summit to the west of this is the summit trig point.

A bad weather descent route to avoid Mickledore, just follow the broken bouldery path north-westerly keeping Dropping Crag on your right, the path feeds down to Lingmell Col then south-westerly to Hollow Stones following well spaced cairns on a grassy meadow until the safety of the stone staircase at Brown Tongue is reached.

MOMMS TIPS

EMERGENCY SLING SEAT HARNESS

An emergency seat harness can be made using a standard 25 mm nylon sling in conjunction with a screwgate karabiner.

Clip the screwgate karabiner into the sling then pass the sling behind the body at waist level (A).

Pass the sling loop with karabiner up through the legs (B) and clip into the two loops of the sling at the front with the karabiner (C) then lock the screwgate.

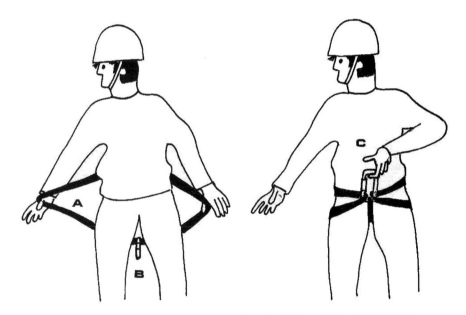

EMERGENCY SLING SEAT HARNESS

*It's Yorkshire's rose our next encounter
three peaks challenge is our quest,
So stride through Dales and look in wonder
at Yorkshire's pride of three of the best.*

THE YORKSHIRE THREE PEAKS

The Yorkshire Three Peaks classic walk takes in the ascents of Pen-y-ghent, Whernside and Ingleborough, usually in that order. Being three of the highest peaks in Yorkshire, they are situated around the headwaters of the river Ribble near the Yorkshire Dales village of Horton in Ribblesdale, just off the B6479 out of Settle.

The walk of some 25 miles should normally take the average mountain walker around 9 to 12 hours to complete and is usually done anticlockwise starting from the Horton in Ribblesdale cafe *(Fig No 4)* where there is a unique clocking in and out machine that registers personal details and starting times of your walk. Remember to clock back in on your return or phone 01729 860333, or you could be reported missing and a search could be initiated.

Pen-y-ghent is the first peak, standing at 2.277 feet above sea level. From the car park at the centre of the village, make your way to the southern end near the church and the Golden Lion pub. Just before the church on your left there is a wooden gate and path, go through the gate and follow the path which brings you to two more wooden gates. Go through these and you'll see a wooden bridge on your left, cross this.

The alternative is to pass the church and go over Horton bridge, turn left up the side road and follow the beck on your left where you'll find the wooden bridge that you would have crossed having gone via the church path.

Passing the school on your right, the road brings you round to an old farm at Brackenbottom where a signpost points the way through the farm yard reading (Pen-y-ghent summit 1¾ miles). Go through the farm yard keeping to the left and over the stile, an uncomplicated route heading east follows the wall side through green fields and limestone ramparts towards Pen-y-ghent on undulating ground. The path takes you up to the very foot of the south ridge where newly laid stone steps (about 80) lead up to a large double step ladder stile. Climb over and turn left, this brings you again to newly laid stone steps which reach upwards.

To Ribblehead & Whernside

To Horton

Lodge Hall

Water

River Ribble

Cattle Grid

Dyke

Bridge

Netherlodge

Bridge

3 Peaks

Swinesett Hill

Great Barn

Gods Bridge

Cow Field

Stone Roller

Brown Gill Beck

Plank Bridge

High Birkwith

Limestone Outcrop

Stream

Old Ing

Dismal Hill

Farm Track

Steps

Gap in wall

Hole in wall

Gate

Dyke

Black Dub Moss

Hull Pot Beck

Rocky Track

Hull Pot

Crown Hotel

Railway Station

Pen y ghent

Bridge

Campsite Cafe

Golden Lion

Horton Beck

School

Penning Way

Wall

Wall Corner

Bogs

Crag

White Path back to Horton

Steps

Cairn

Steps

Boulderfield Staircase

Pen - y - Ghent 2277 ft

Limestone Ramp

Boulders

Brackenbottom

Horton in Ribblesdale

Not to scale

16

THE YORKSHIRE THREE PEAKS

A shaly path feeds you onto a natural set of limestone steps that peter out onto large rock blocks. The path levels off and leads you to a large boulderfield, pick your way up through the boulders onto an easily found but steep path staircase. Again a final rocky scramble takes you up onto the lower grassy plateau where a large path leads directly to the summit, with the stone wall on the left a simple stroll brings you up to the summit trig point at 2.277 feet.

The wall on the summit, running from the south to the north-east, offers a good wind shelter and by climbing over the ladder stile a windbreak can be found on either side.

From the summit, having crossed the wooden ladder, walk straight on slightly to the right. At about 50 metres there is a large cairn, then stone steps leading down to a very obvious path, that follows the western edge of Pen-y-ghent. Descend to the crag on your right, from here the path splits into two with the main path running downhill on your left. This looks white in colour and leads back to Horton in Ribblesdale, while the other path which is less obvious, runs down to the right through the wet and boggy ground heading for the wall corner where a high wooden ladder stile leads you over the wall.

Again erosion has played it's part on this section, leaving the ground raked with wet and boggy areas until a white bouldery path rises over the hill and another ladder stile brings you to the Hull Pot Beck. Cross this and proceed on wet ground again up over towards Black Dub Moss Moor until a wooden gate brings you to a deep dyke, which is best crossed upstream.

Continue over the moor through a broken wall in the general direction of the Ribblehead viaduct, up and over another small hill the path drops down to where the path, stream and wall meet. Go through the gap in the wall, eventually you will come to another wall with steps, cross this and over the next hill to where you'll find green fields and good solid ground where the path peters out onto a farmer's track.

Follow the track until a large gate is reached, there is a small wood dropping down a ravine to the left and a little farm house just below the hill on the right. Pass the gate and proceed to the T-junction, then walk straight across the road onto a grassy meadow and down to a small stream with two railway sleepers as a bridge. Continue up over a small grassy hillock and down the track running parallel with a wall.

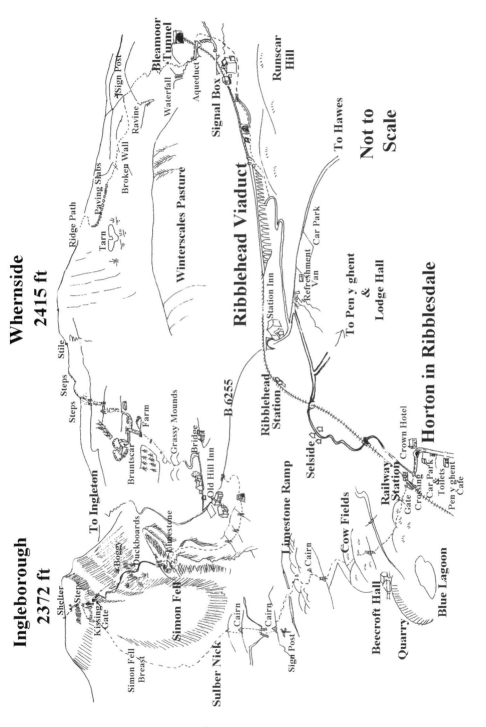

THE YORKSHIRE THREE PEAKS

Climb over a set of stone steps and continue to follow the track until it begins to turn right (be careful here as it's easy to lose your way), a stone roller marks the way. Follow the wall on your left straight on through what's normally a cow field, there are two large stone boulders in the field and at the far end the natural feature of Godsbridge.

Over the stile at Godsbridge and turn left onto a track passing the old barn on your left, eventually the track leads to a ladder stile and bridge at Netherlodge. A large signpost with the words "Three Peaks" painted in white marks the way, cross the bridge and keep to the right passing between the main farm house and the old barn. On the left a ladder stile takes you to a small road, turn left and follow the road, eventually crossing the river Ribble.

Continue on the road crossing a dyke and then a cattle grid, the road takes a clockwise sharp bend (please keep to the road here) and passes close to an old house (Lodge Hall) at Ingham Lodge dating back to 1687. Further on the road on your left is a water trough before the road swings left and uphill to the main Horton to Ribblehead road.

Turn right on the main road and try to face oncoming traffic. Walk for a mile until the junction at Ribblehead is reached, cross the road and head straight for the viaduct which has 24 arches. Built in 1875 the Ribblehead viaduct railway bridge links up the Settle and Carlisle railways. Keep to the right of the arches (the path runs parallel with the railway track).

Follow the path up over a brow, just before a culvert there is a large information board about the three peaks. The track now runs up to a large gate then onwards until an old signal box and ruined house are reached, the track is undulating and made with railway ballast which makes walking awkward.

A small stream is crossed (don't be tempted to cross the small bridge on your left) just keep on the track until you come across a wide stream with stepping stones, cross this the best you can. Ahead on your left there is an aqueduct over the railway, the track crosses this to a stile at the far end.

On your right the railway line disappears into the tunnel at Bleamoor, a stony path now rises steeply up until reaching another stile with views of the Force Gill waterfall. The obvious path runs up the hillside in large zigzags then straightens out reaching towards Deepdale.

19

THE YORKSHIRE THREE PEAKS

Push on upwards, passing a ravine on the moor to your left, until a three-pronged signpost is reached. Turn left and over the stile for Whernside, follow the path slowly rising until a broken wall is reached, carry on over a steep rise keeping the broken wall on your right until the paving stone section. The paving slabs give way to a steep and broken section of path at the start of the ridge, on your left is a small tarn.

Follow the ridge path keeping to the wall on your right until at the summit the wall dog-legs out about two metres, this is the true summit, an opening in the wall gives access to the trig point, Whernside 2,415 feet.

Back onto the path again keeping the wall on your right, continue until the ground falls away steeply towards a wire fence. Cross the stile here then follow the path straight onwards, again a steep drop onto man-made steps and the path levels off before dropping steeply to the left, the path branches off the ridge and down a very steep set of rocky steps (be careful here it's steep) until a double ladder stile is reached.

Still steep, the path now worms down a grassy bank to a large gate with a ladder stile on either side, this brings you into a more gentle descent through a cow field until a barn and small lane are reached. Go down the lane branching right passing a large set of boulders on your right. Here there is what appears to be a fireplace set deep into the wall side, the path turns left with a Hill Inn signpost pointing the way.

Now on a tarmac road the walking is easy, pass the farm on the left and a series of cattle grids and fields through rolling countryside. There is a large wood on your right, the road snakes it's way through mounds of grassy meadows before dropping down over a bridge and swinging right onto Philpin Lane, slowly rising past a farm and Philpin House up onto the main Ingleton to Hawes road, turn left to find the Hill Inn, a welcome break with refreshment at hand (don't over do it!).

Having rested and sampled the refreshments to be had, drag yourself away from the warmth of the open wood fire and again brave the elements.

On your way out, at the main door turn right and walk up the hill for 150 yards to a new gate on the right hand side, a good track swings to the right passing a stone built arched culvert on your left and an information plaque on your right.

THE YORKSHIRE THREE PEAKS

Follow the path over a series of fields and ladder stiles keeping the limestone escarpment to your left until the ground begins to rise and works it's way through the river of limestone rocks that protect Ingleborough's northerly approach. This well used track snakes it's way to a double ladder stile passing a large crater on your left called Braithwaite Wife Hole. From here onwards, the path is of wooden duck boards placed to protect the boggy moorland from erosion, it rises steeply at first then drops into a hollow before steeply rising with a vengeance until the stone steps at the base of Ingleborough are reached.

These broken steps steeply edge up vertically swinging slightly to the left and then to the right, finishing at an open gully where a swing gate can be found. Go through this and climb the steps to a cairn which marks the junction for the return path route to Horton in Ribblesdale on your left.

The path now rises over broken ground up over a small outcrop topped with two cairns, continuing onto the summit plateau heading directly ahead about 240 degrees until the summit four-way shelter is reached and a welcome rest can be had.

In thick misty conditions an 80 degree bearing from the shelter will bring you safely back to the two cairns protecting the outcrop. Retrace the path down to the steps until a single cairn marking the route to Horton is reached, then turn right downhill at an approx bearing of 104 degrees south-east over Simon Fell Breast.

Follow the path for approx. 2½ miles to Sulber Nick, Pen-y-ghent can be seen on the horizon in front of you and down in the valley bottom lies Horton in Ribblesdale, there is a large cairn at the end of Sulber Nick where the path drops down to a double step ladder stile. Drop down further passing another cairn and a signpost pointing out the route to Austwick and Horton, the path now is limestone under foot. Proceed through the broken wall over the limestone scar outcroppings following yellow topped posts down to a ladder stile.

You arrive back into grassy meadows surrounded by sheep but sadly the ground under foot is wet and boggy. Follow the wall round to the right and cross the field, another ladder stile brings you to the quarry access road which you cross. On your right is Beecroft Hall Farm, walk straight on following the path across a steep bank to a gate, and on the right are views of the quarry and blue lagoon.

Continue over the field and through another gate where steps take you down to the railway crossing, be careful here, look and listen.

Cross the track when clear and walk down to the main road, straight on and turn right over the bridge which brings you to the car park and toilets. Remember to clock out at the cafe or you could be reported missing and a search could be initiated.

Fig No 4

The Pen-y-ghent cafe in Horton in Ribblesdale

Views of Mont Blanc

Fig No 5

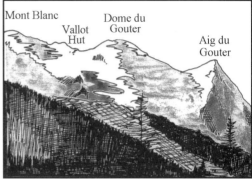

View of Mont Blanc from Chamonix

The Nid De Aigle Restaurant

Lower arete leading to the Tete Rousse glacier

Fig No 6

Fig No 7

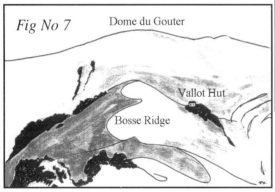

The Dome du Gouter seen from the Tournette Ridge

We switch from Dales to Alpine prize
12,000 feet we aim to rise,
So take a chance to stand upon
the very summit of Mont Blanc.

A 12,000 FOOT PEAK

Because Britain does not have a peak as high as 12,000 feet, the obvious place to look would be the European Alps, be it Switzerland or France the range of mountains to choose from is endless of course, so the Momms have adopted the Mont Blanc range. The equivalent height on any other mountain be it Mount Teide on Tenerife or some obscure mountain in the Himalayas would suffice and the Momms feat is yours to claim.

The Aiguille du Gouter on the "Route Normale" on Mont Blanc would be enough to claim the feat. Also the opportunity to climb Mont Blanc, the highest mountain in the west of Europe is only a stones throw away, but sadly many attempts have been frustrated by a combination of poor preparation and incorrect approach, so the following route guide and tips will uncover the mysteries of both peaks.

Mont Blanc the highest mountain in the west of modern Europe still exercises a great magnetism for mountaineers of all ages, perhaps greater than any other mountain in the world. I have made seven successful ascents of the Gouter route normally accompanying small groups of mountaineering friends and still find the ascent exciting and as rewarding as my first ascent in 1980.

The Gouter route or Normal route is technically easy but nevertheless still very dangerous. The excitement of crossing the Grand Couloir, the exhilarating scramble up the Gouter ridge, the final climb up into the sunrise with the awe inspiring magnificent scenery and finally the exposed summit ridge makes this perhaps the finest snow route in the Alps.

I hope that the following chapter will clear some of the mysteries for those intent on ascending, and increase the likelihood of success. Remember August 1998 when 22 people died on Mont Blanc in one week and most on the "Route Normale".

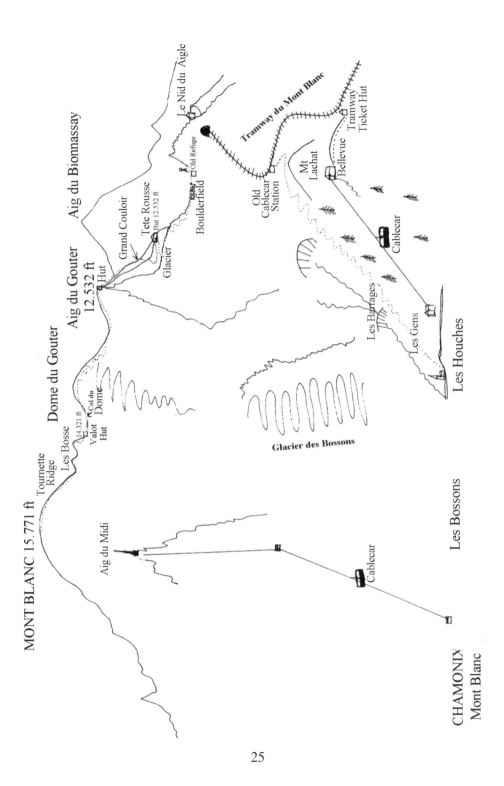

MONT BLANC 15.771 ft

Tournette Ridge

Les Bosse

Dome du Gouter

Aig du Gouter 12.532 ft

Aig du Bionnassay

Le Nid du Aigle

Tramway du Mont Blanc

Bellevue
Tramway Ticket Hut

Mt Lachat

Old Cablecar Station

Old Refuge

Boulderfield

Tete Rousse
Hut 12.532 ft

Grand Couloir

Glacier

Hut

Col du Dome

Valot Hut
14.321 ft

Les Barrages

Les Gens

Cablecar

Les Houches

Glacier des Bossons

Aig du Midi

Cablecar

Les Bossons

CHAMONIX
Mont Blanc

A 12,000 FOOT PEAK

THE FIRST DAY:

ROUTES TO THE NID D'AIGLE (Eagles Nest)

There are three alternative ways to start the ascent of Mont Blanc, by the Gouter/Bosse Ridge route (Route Normale).

The main aim is to reach the Nid du Aigle view point above the Bionnassay Glacier, this is where the climb really starts. *(Fig No 5)*

Firstly, there is the Tramway du Mont Blanc train which can be caught at St Gervais and will take you up to the Nid du Aigle view point.

Secondly, from Les Houches the cablecar will take you up to within a short walk of the Tramway du Mont Blanc train stop point, here the train can be caught to the Nid du Aigle view point.

Thirdly, at the end of the climbing season both train and cable car will be closed and the natural route from Les Houches must be taken by foot. Walk up the road behind the church in the centre of Les Houches to Les Gens. Take the footpath up the ridge in the forest via the old cable car station then follow the railway track up to the Nid du Aigle restaurant and railway station view point.

To the Tete Rousse Hut 10.398 ft (2 to 3 hours):

From the Nid du Aigle view point the path is well marked in red paint as well as signposted. 100 metres up the path from the station turn left where a steep zigzag path takes you up through the desert du Pierre - Ronde, passing a large metal beacon on the left hand side. There is a steep rock section with metal fittings to aid climbing, otherwise it's just a straight forward walk up to the old refuge at Baraque Forestiere, turn right over a small boulder field and feed onto the lower Arete leading to the Tete Rousse glacier. *(Fig No 6)*

Nearing the top of the ridge the Tete Rousse hut comes into view on your upper right side perched on the edge of a now receding Tete Rousse glacier. The glacier angle at the top of the ridge is steep and littered with water filled crevasses. It may pay to climb 150 metres further up and cross the glacier wearing crampons. The hut stands at an altitude of 10,398 feet and contains 68 beds, It has a guardian from mid June to the end of September and remember reservations for hut places are compulsory, telephone 045 09 93 95 91.

A 12,000 FOOT PEAK

In the hut a hot dinner and breakfast can be booked, there are blankets on the beds and the toilets can be tricky to reach in bad weather but there are splendid views of the Bionnassay north face and beautiful sunsets.

THE SECOND DAY:

TO THE GOUTER HUT 12,476 ft

From the Tete Rousse hut cross the upper glacier to the left, the track will arch round to the right hand side and become very steep. Leave the glacier and move onto a well trodden shale path which zigzags up to the start of the Grand Couloir. On the left hand side approach watch out for verglass ice on the lower rock scramble, the centre of the couloir is raked with constant rock fall and is extremely dangerous. Always wear a helmet and move safely and quickly across until the safety of the lower arete on the other side is gained.

The Gouter Ridge seen from the Tete Rousse hut looks daunting to say the least but once the Grand Couloir is crossed and the initial climb onto good rock at the foot of the ridge is made, we can now break down the ridge into five distinctive sections, the first section is a scramble, come walk, on a broken well marked path which turns the first major buttress on the right hand side.

The second and third sections are good enjoyable rock scrambling, try to follow the red paint marks avoiding loose rocks on the left hand side that can fall down on fellow climbers who are crossing the couloir below. The fourth section again becomes more of a broken path which leads to the fifth and final section of steep rock, fixed ropes, and metal ladders. Expect queues here.

The route brings you out in front of the aluminium made hut at 12,476 feet, the main entrance door to the hut is on your left hand side, walk through a usually dark storage area for rucksacks and boots and turn right up the stairs to the main room, you will be welcomed at the counter.

The hut holds 168 beds and remember reservations are compulsory for all huts, ring the Guardian of the Gouter hut on 0450 54 40 93 to book. In an emergency it's possible to sleep on the floor but it's not recommended. Out of the hut turn left and follow the patio to the top corner, here you can sunbathe on seats and find cubicle toilets which are located down the steps. To the rear of the hut next to the new annexe the path takes you up the snow ramp about 15 feet into a new world of snow and ice with splendid views all round.

Shutlingsloe

Trevor Atkinson

Mont Blanc depicting the Valot Hut and Bosse Ridge

A 12,000 FOOT PEAK

Remember to fit crampons and take your ice axe, the ramp brings you onto the lower ridge so turn right and follow the path, a short climb and walk brings you onto the summit of the Aiguille du Gouter at 12,532 feet, your Momms is gained.

THE THIRD DAY:

Dinner is usually served between 6pm and 7pm, with the excitement of the forthcoming ascent, the altitude and the noise it will be virtually impossible to sleep. The hut lights come on about 2.30 am and there's a mad scramble for pre booked breakfasts.

Weather permitting it is best to climb up the ramp at the back of the hut before roping up, this will give you more room to move and think. The route again follows the corniced ridge up over the Aiguille du Gouter, the track is well trodden and impossible to miss. Try to keep a steady slow pace while climbing up the Dome du Gouter for it's a long hard slog and is easy to burn yourself out.

Having climbed the Dome the route descends into the Col du Dome before climbing steeply up to the Vallot hut. The hut stands at 14,321 feet and is usually approached from the rear due to it's position being perched on a rocky buttress. Climb up the ladder to gain entry, remember this hut is an emergency hut and has a radiophone inside, also overnighting at this altitude without acclimatisation can be fatal.

This is probably the coldest part of the climb, day light on the horizon around 6am and a very steep pull up the Grand Bosse Ridge that leads onto the Petite Bosse and hopefully the first rays of the sun. Watch out for crevasses and keep well clear of any corniced edges, possibly the most dangerous place on the mountain comes next. *(Fig No 7)*

Between the Bosse Ridge and the start of the Tournette Ridge, the ridge narrows to an icy path about a foot wide. Take care here for there's not much protection and virtually impossible to get an ice axe in to hold a fall. Follow the ridge up passing many false horizons and would be summits, this is where you have to fight the altitude and use every ounce of determination left in your body. The last part of the summit ridge is very exposed but that's soon forgotten when the summit expanse is finally reached and Mont Blanc is yours for that moment in time, Mont Blanc 15,771 feet. Remember to take care on the descent, this is where accidents happen.

A12,000 FOOT PEAK

A ROUGH GUIDE TO WHAT, WHY AND WHEN

Equipment List:

Ice axe	Required on Tete Rousse glacier, Gouter ridge and summit.
Crampons	Required on Tete Rousse glacier, Gouter ridge and summit.
Harness	Required on Tete Rousse glacier, Gouter ridge and summit.
Rope 11mm	Required on the Grand Couloir and summit bid.
Sunglasses	Required for crossing glaciers.
Ski Goggles	Required for summit bid, protection in high winds.
Mittens	A must for summit bid, mittens keep fingers warm.
Gaiters	Required, often deep melted snow on descent.
Water bottle	Very important, no water until the Gouter hut, drink plenty.
Cooking gear	For melting snow & cooking food, end of hut season.
Head lamp	Required for summit bid & toilet trips, also spare bulb.
Helmet	A must for crossing the Grand Couloir both ways.
Duvet Jacket	A must for summit bid, balaclava for intense cold.
Camera	A must.
Book	A must for sitting around in the hut.

Iolo Jones
(founder member, climber
& fell runner)

Mickledore Pass
and Scafell Crag

Tryfan's North Ridge

THE MOMMS POEM

There comes a time to take a chance
with skill and nerve and high romance,
We Mom we climb to show our mettle
feat not achieved thou need not settle,
We travel high we travel low
our quest starts on Shutlingsloe.

To earn the badge just come along
endure the challenge of the Mom,
Ben Nevis to climb and conquer
and Snowdon falls before our feet,
These we climb with passion
on Scafell Pike summit we aim to meet.

It's Yorkshire's rose our next encounter
three peaks challenge is our quest,
So stride through Dales and look in wonder
at Yorkshire's pride of three of the best..

We switch from Dales to Alpine prize
12,000 feet we aim to rise,
So take a chance to stand upon
the very summit of Mont Blanc,
The Welsh XIV are not to be missed
and climb Jack's Rake we must insist.

North ridge of Tryfan with Adam & Eve
stride the gap to succeed,
With freedom taken aim for Bristly
the mighty ridge you'll scale so quickly,
Cross the portals of Castell y Gwynt too
it's time for Snowdonia's famous Horseshoe.

A technical climb of 300 feet
climb the rock face and don't be beat,
If you abseil down to descend
use figure of eight it will be your friend,
On Pen Yr Ole Wen's great face of Braich ty du
climb the Pinnacle for all to see.
Then finally make your way down
to the boozer in the nearby town.

A celebratory drink is on the agenda
call at the Vic in nearby Bethesda,
And reflect on those who've lied
The curse of the Momms will decide
Of what fate that will become
The liar, the cheat, the spineless one.

THE MOMMS BADGE

1	Ben Nevis	7	North Ridge Tryfan
2	Snowdon	8	Bristly Ridge
3	Scafell Pike	9	Technical Ability
4	Yorkshire 3 Peaks	10	Adam & Eve
5	12,000 Foot Peak	11	Castell y Gwynt
6	XIV Welsh 3000	12	Braich ty du Pinnacle

Fig No 1

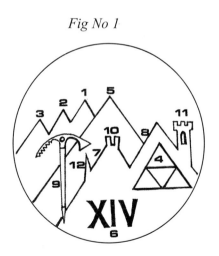

Not shown on the Momms Badge are Shutingsloe
Snowdon Horseshoe and Jack's Rake.

Rock climbing and Abseiling come under No 9 Technical Ability.

MOMMS TIPS

COMPASS

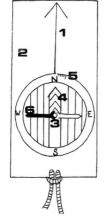

The
Protractor
Compass

1 **Large Direction Arrow**

2 **Base Plate**

3 **Compass needle pivot point**

4 **Housing Arrow with north - south lines**

5 **Rotating Housing with degree markings**

6 **Compass needle**

TAKING A BEARING

As well as setting the map with the lay of the land the map can also be set with a compass, place the compass on the map, turn the map until the north south lines of the map are aligned with the needle of the compass pointing north.

Place the edge of your compass on your direct line of travel, align the rotating housing arrow (4) with the north / south grid lines on the map, simply read off the bearing (5) for the direction you wish to take.

Add the appropriate magnetic variation for the area you are in, FROM GRID TO MAG ADD. Magnetic variation varies with time and place, an exact variation will be given on the map legend, the current variation for 2002 is approximately 4° west of grid north.

Follow the magnetic bearing indicated by the large direction arrow (1), hold the compass in front of you with the large direction arrow pointing directly away from you, turn your body until the red compass needle (6) falls within the housing arrow (4), then walk in the direction of the large arrow (1). Pick out one or more features in your line of travel and simply walk to them, repeating the process to keep on course.

Brian Smith
(climber & Momms
website designer)

Straddle move on Jack's Rake. Pavey Ark

Cannon rock on Tryfan North Ridge

Brian Smith on the cantilever rock on Glyder Fach

Berwyn Williams leaping Adam & Eve Stones on the summit of Tryfan.

THE WELSH XIV

To walk the Welsh three thousand foot challenge is a feat in itself, this is where the Momms endurance test raises it's painful head. All told there are fourteen peaks that make up the Momms Welsh 3,000, the newly re-surveyed Carnedd Uchaf which is gained with minimum effort and is merely a point on the landscape and is not considered in the Momms challenge. The Momms peaks are as follows lying from the south to the north for 27 miles with approximately 11,000 feet of ascent.

SNOWDON Yr Wyddfa 3,560 ft
CRIB-Y-DDYSGL 3,493 ft
CRIB GOCH 3,026 ft

ELIDIR FAWR 3,029 ft
Y-GARN 3,104 ft
GLYDER FAWR 3,279 ft
GLYDER FACH 3,262 ft
TRYFAN 3,010 ft

PEN YR OLE WEN 3,210 ft
CARNEDD DAFYDD 3,426 ft
CARNEDD LLEWELYN 3,484 ft
YR ELEN 3,152 ft
FOEL GRACH 3,195 ft
FOEL FRAS 3,091 ft

The Welsh XIV can be broken down into three main areas, these are, the Snowdon range consisting of Snowdon, Crib y Ddysgl (Carnedd Ugain) and Crib Goch.

The Glyderau consisting of Elidir Fawr, Y Garn, Glyder Fawr, Glyder Fach and Tryfan.

The Carneddau consisting of Pen yr Ole Wen, Carnedd Dafydd, Carnedd Llewelyn, Yr Elen, Foel Grach and Foel Fras.

THE WELSH XIV

It is suggested that all three mountain ranges of the Welsh XIV be reconnoitred and made familiar before attempting the full 27 miles of the XIV peaks 3000 challenge.

The following is just a brief description of the route and not a working guide, so remember the best time to take up the challenge is mid summer, hopefully you will have dry weather and long hours of daylight to help guide you on your way.

At about 11.00 p.m. start from Pen-y-Pass and take the Pyg track route to the summit of Snowdon via Bwlch Moch (described in Snowdon ascent) it is usual to bivouac on the summit of Snowdon until 2.30 am, this guarantees you some semblance of early day break when approaching Crib Goch in summer time at least, from the summit follow the path that runs parallel with the railway down to the monolith stone at Bwlch Glas.

Passing the monolith veer off to the right upwards towards Crib y Ddysgl (Carnedd Ugain) at 3,495 feet, then onwards on the undulating and exciting ridge in the half light of the new day until the pinnacles of Crib Goch are reached (see illustration in Snowdon Horseshoe).

On reaching Crib Goch secondary summit at 3,023 feet at the far end of the knife edge ridge, proceed down via the steep north ridge for about half a mile, balancing the ridge between Cwm Uchat and Cwm Beudy-Mawr. The end of the ridge is defended by the fortress crags of Dinas Mot , to avoid this a westward steep scree path is descended into Cwm Glas Mawr then follow the stream down to the A4086 at Blaen y nant, turn left down the hill towards Llanberis and walk for one and a half miles until the quaint village of Nant Peris is reached.

The alternative route for the more adventurous would be to climb up from Pen y Pass to Crib Goch via Bwlch Moch using the Pyg track, before climbing and traversing Crib Goch using head torches (see Snowdon horseshoe). Then continuing along the ridge until Crib y Ddysgl (Carnedd Ugain) is reached. Descend down to Bwlch Glas turn left passing the monolith stone and follow the path running parallel with the railway up to the summit of Snowdon before reversing the route until Clogwyn station. Turn right down the steep grassy bank (be careful in wet weather) into Cwm Glas Bach, the grassy bank leads into a scree gully and eventually a twisting path follows the stream downwards heading for a cottage. Here an access lane leads to the A4086 via a small bridge, turn left at the road and Nant Peris is half a mile away.

There is a large car park and toilets in Nant Peris which make an ideal place to make a rendezvous with your back up team.

Braich Ty Du Pinnacle, below the slopes of Pen yr Ole Wen

Bristly Ridge, showing Great Pinnacle Gap

Prominent Pinnacle at the end of Jack's Rake

Pavey Ark

Walk down the road from the car park and just before the chapel on the right at G.R. 606584 turn right, follow the lane bearing left, a signpost points the way. Watch out for the stile on the right hand side, above lies Elidir Fawr, a name you will not forget in a hurry.

Continue upwards over a ladder stile and through an iron gate until you reach a footbridge, you'll find it quite wet under foot and one hell of a slog. Head due north up a broad grassy bank. A boulder raked summit with a welcoming wind shelter awaits you, Elidir Fawr 3,029 feet is yours.

From the summit of Elidir Fawr heading north-east follow cairns over rocky ground until a good broad path on a grassy ridge is reached.

Continue following the now narrowing ridge in a clockwise arch passing Bwlch y Breacan and the outstanding peak of Foel Goch on the left until you get to grips with the loose and shaly path. Ascending the steep slopes of Y Garn, your fifth peak, standing at the height of 3,104 feet. A rocky path now descends steeply to a small mountain tarn at Llyn y Cwn, here an emergency escape route down to Ogwen Valley via the Devil's Kitchen can be found, but for those on the MOMMS quest, to the left of the tarn facing Glyder Fawr a small rocky gully is followed upwards until a path heading slightly south-east is reached, eventually arriving on a rocky barren plateau where the summit can be found at 3,279 feet.

Now head eastwards bearing 75 degrees, following numerous cairns you descend a little into Bwlch y Ddwy Glyder before being confronted with the Castell y Gwynt, *Fig No 8* (Castle of the Winds), a large mass of spiny rock shapes guarding the approaches to Glyder Fach which may be turned by descending to the right hand side, thus losing height and time, or climbed the MOMMS style. Tackle the rocks directly and have fun, so don't waste too much time for Glyder Fach awaits you at 3,262 feet. Take the steep shaly gullies of the Bristly Ridge path (not scramble) to descend, then swinging north-east towards a rewarding scramble up onto Tryfan summit 3,010 feet before descending down the south-west gully to the road below. Time to rest your knees here at Llyn Ogwen and be welcomed by your back up teams once more.

THE WELSH XIV

If you stand facing Llyn Ogwen, directly in front of you stands Pen yr Ole Wen, walk to the right and at the far end of the lake at Pont Tal y Llyn a small lane leads to the left passing a shaded wooded area. Cross the small bridge and follow the lane until the well marked footpath leads upwards, following the Afon Lloer watercourse before entering the basin of Cwm Lloer with it's picturesque tarn of Ffynnon Lloer.

Branch off to the left to the lower ridge where a short wet scramble brings you onto a long hot slog along a never ending ridge, (it's time for shorts). Eventually you will reach the plateau and summit of Pen yr Ole Wen at 3,211 feet. From here head north-east and follow the natural line of the mountain, an easy walk brings you to Carnedd Dafydd at 3,423 feet and a restful wind shelter.

Now follow the obvious path eastwards above the Black Ladders rock face arching northerly up to Carnedd Llewelyn at 3,485 the highest of the Carneddau. A short detour now heading about NW some 285 degrees, a steep descent down a winding path and a climb up onto a grassy summit of Yr Elen at 3,152 feet before returning back onto the Llewelyn plateau and heading north-east until the main track is found. The wide ridge heads N.N.E. A slight descent and then a slow rise brings you to Foel Grach at 3,195 feet.

Hidden away just to the north-east of the summit amongst the crags is a mountain refuge shelter, drop down from Foel Grach onto open wind swept moorland. Bypass the newly surveyed Carnedd Uchaf and keep it to your left, head northwards at about 15 degrees until you reach a stone-ridge wall. Follow this never ending wall until the last and most isolated summit is reached, Foel Fras at 3,091 feet. Well done! the MOMMS XIV is yours, all you have to do now is retrace your footsteps along the wall and pick up the track heading west between Carnedd Uchaf and Yr Aryg and a painful descent down the grassy slopes into Cwm Caseg where a path leads you down into Gerlan and Bethesda.

Fig No 8

Castell y Gwynt

Iolo Jones on
Braich Ty du Pinnacle

The Summit Shelter
on the Summit of Ben Nevis

Ingleborough one of the Yorkshire Three Peaks

and climb Jack's Rake we must insist

JACK'S RAKE

Jack's Rake of the MOMMS poem refers to the rock fault known as Jack's Rake that runs across the mighty crag of Pavey Ark. From Ambleside in the Lake District take the A593 as far as Skelwith Bridge and follow the signs for Great Langdale on the B5343 as far as the New Dungeon Ghyll Hotel. There is a car park across from the hotel that hides away in the shadows of the elegant looking Langdale pikes above.

At the back of the New Dungeon Ghyll Hotel a foot path edges it's way up to the left of Stickle Ghyll, passing numerous waterfalls and crosses a bridge that spans the Ghyll. The path zigzags a little and then becomes steep to the right of the largest waterfall where a broken rocky path leads upwards, the path levels out a little until the Ghyll is crossed once more on stepping stones. The path then weaves it's way up through boulders to where Stickle Tarn is reached.

Situated in a magnificent position to the north west of the Tarn stands the intimidating rock face of Pavey Ark. On closer examination a well defined fault cuts diagonally across the crag from right to left and follows a rocky trough for most of the way, thus concealing the exposure of the lower cliff until the final stages of the climb. Jack's Rake is graded as an easy rock climb and is quite exposed and in places lethal to the unwary in icy or wet conditions.

Walk around the edge of Stickle Tarn in a clockwise direction to the far side, a broken path cuts upwards through a small boulder field then continues up the scree passing a large cairn monument marked J.S.W. 1900.

The scree path brings you up to the lower part of the main crag where Jack's Rake meets Easy Gully. A grassy start leads onto a rocky ramp of easy climbing, slowly edging into a steep rock groove which is a natural drainage in wet weather. Pass the first ash tree (now dead) at the bottom of Rake End Chimney and climb upwards passing the second ash tree. The next fifty yards is the steepest and worst section of the steep rock groove, made easy by edging a little to the left hand of the outer rim of the parapet that protects from the exposure of the rock face below.

The third ash tree offers a welcome rest, the path turns slightly right and easier climbing up to Gwynne's Chimney, now a downward traverse brings you to the next steep groove. Care should be taken here for it is the most dangerous part of the route.

Extremely exposed just above a large tree an awkward start to gain the groove is made by straddling with the left foot and a large left hand jug hold to step up into the groove. Then straight forward climbing up the steep groove for ten yards to turn the cannon shaped rock *(Fig No 9)* then onto easy terrace, which brings another rock groove of broken easier rock where Great Gully is reached.

The route is nearly in the bag now, but be careful not to lose the route here, turn right picking your way upwards. A left hand traverse to an open area with big rock steps.

Climb directly up the rock steps and up steep slabs, or continue downwards slightly on a climber's path for a few yards (be careful here in wet weather). Climb up easily towards the pointed pinnacle aiming for the depression on the right. Find the summit wall within 15 yards and climb rocks to the right, from here the summit lies some 100 yards further on. Pavey Arch 2,288ft.

Descend to Stickle Tarn by North Rake or continue on to climb Harrison's Stickle 2,403ft. and Pike o Stickle 2,323ft.

Fig No 9   **Looking down the Rake from the cannon shaped rock.**

JACK'S RAKE ON PAVEY ARK

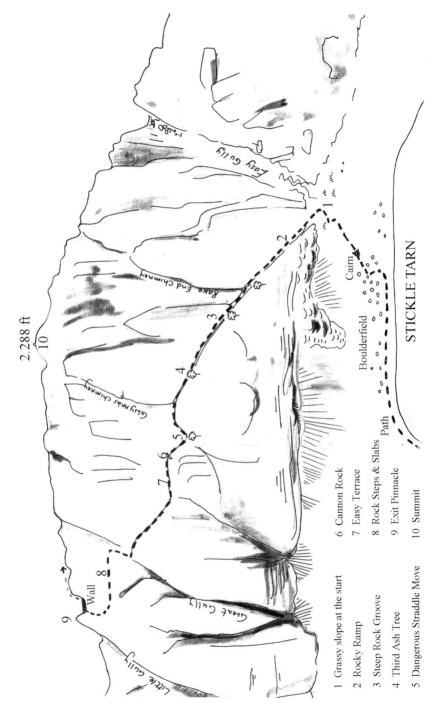

2.288 ft

1 Grassy slope at the start
2 Rocky Ramp
3 Steep Rock Groove
4 Third Ash Tree
5 Dangerous Straddle Move

6 Cannon Rock
7 Easy Terrace
8 Rock Steps & Slabs
9 Exit Pinnacle
10 Summit

STICKLE TARN

46

NORTH RIDGE OF TRYFAN

Tryfan, on the eastern banks of Llyn Ogwen, next to the A5 (T) road that runs south-eastwards out of Bethesda towards Capel Curig, stands proud and dominant at 3,010 feet guarding the northern approaches of the Glyderau against the mild and timid of heart who fear the height and dragons above, for Tryfan with it's splendid pyramid shape is guarded on all sides by rock with it's more prominent north ridge trailing down from the summit to the very shores of Llyn Ogwen.

This is where we start our climb, there is ample parking space in the lay-bys and car park that can be found hidden away amongst the boulders at the foot of Milestone buttress G.R.663603, either from the car park or the steps of the lay-by, make your way up to the foot Milestone buttress which is a prominent feature on the lower west side of the north ridge of Tryfan. A dry stone wall runs up from the lay-by to the rock face, this is the starting point.

From the car park, pass through the metal gate at the far eastern end, over a small boulder field and a steep scramble brings you up to the dry stone wall. Cross using the ladder steps, on the left side of the wall climb upwards over broken ground keeping the rock face on your right, carefully passing up through scree and loose rocks to the first heather col, passing ash trees on your right.

Don't be tempted to break too early for the right hand ridge, for it is protected by wet and loose heather terraces with huge rock stoppers. Climb the screes until a prominent buttress on the far left is reached, where a Y-gully can be found. Break to the left side and easy steps take you onto the screes above and eventually a prominent sheep track runs to the right just below rocky ramparts. Scale these until the 'Cannon', a famous rock feature, is found over on the right.

Continue along the rocky crest until the next high barrier is reached, keep to the left and enjoy an interesting scramble up the boulders. Continue to the next large platform below a prominent nose of rock, again an entertaining scramble up polished rock to a subsidiary summit. Via a notch in the ridge continue to the north summit where the standing stones of Adam and Eve come into view on the main central summit. This is an opportunity to bag yet another of the MOMMS feats, with the verse of ......

"Stride the gap to succeed"

47

North Ridge of Tryfan

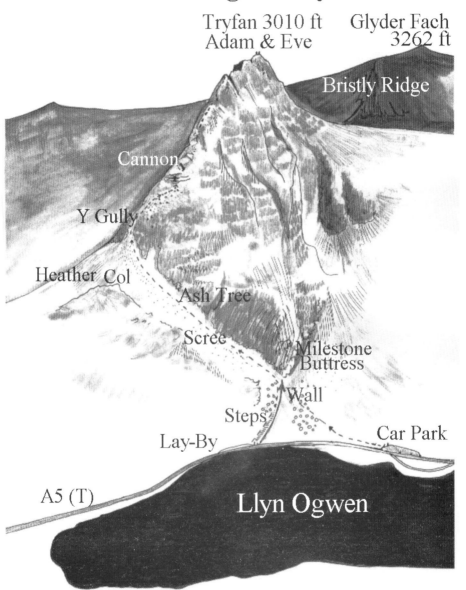

Tryfan 3010 ft
Adam & Eve

Glyder Fach
3262 ft

Bristly Ridge

Cannon

Y Gully

Heather Col

Ash Tree

Scree

Milestone
Buttress

Wall

Steps

Lay-By

Car Park

A5 (T)

Llyn Ogwen

With freedom taken aim for Bristly
the mighty ridge you'll scale so quickly

NORTH RIDGE OF TRYFAN

Be sure to use a bit of common sense here, if it's wet or windy there's always another day, the stones will wait for you and then the freedom of the mountain will be yours so legend says.

Trusting you've been successful, traverse to the south summit and follow the ridge down on it's west side, down to Bwlch Tryfan (the col). Keep to the right of the stone wall that runs between Tryfan and Bristly Ridge at the head of the col.

The link between Tryfan and Glyder Fach via the col (Bwlch Tryfan). Below the south ridge is the spectacular spiny ridge called Bristly Ridge, which provides excellent scrambling with a real sense of exposure with it's steep gullies and rocky gendarme pinnacles.

From the col follow the steep zigzagging path up to the base of the lowest part of the crags above. Some 30 feet up over broken rock to the left is a prominent gully with what looks like a man-made wall at it's base, "This is the key to the route," when you reach the wall you'll find that it's nothing more than a man-made base for the platform above.

This is superb scrambling on mixed ground so take your time and watch for good holds. The lower part of the steep gully suffers from drainage problems in bad weather but improves with height, so go up the initial steep gully until easier ground is found. Continue up the narrowing exposed ridge and over a small pinnacle onto a larger one, then descend into a prominent notch keeping to the left, this is Great Pinnacle Gap. *(Fig No 10)*

Pass through the gap to the right of the pinnacle and regain the jagged crest of the ridge, rising without deviation to easier ground onto a large boulder field that leads to the summit plateau above. Walk south-west to join the normal ascent path passing through the lunar landscape of rocks and boulders.

Follow the path passing close by the 'Cantilever'. This precariously perched slab stands some 100 metres short of the summit of Glyder Fach, 3262 feet. About 300 metres south-west protecting the approaches to Glyder Fawr and the Y Gribin Ridge lies the Castell-y-Gwynt (Castle of the Winds) and castle of your MOMMS.

49

NORTH RIDGE OF TRYFAN

This stockade of portal splinters, monoliths of slab and boulder is every bit a castle. There is no set route across it so just explore and have fun .... be careful.   By traversing to Glyder Fawr and dropping down to Llyn-y-Cwn, a well worn path descends down passing the Devil's Kitchen into Cwm Idwal and the Ogwen Valley.

Fig No 10

THE SNOWDON HORSESHOE

One of the finest ridge traverses in the country it provides an excellent day out, a real test of endurance and nerve. The Snowdon Horseshoe can be broken down into four main sections, with the first being Crib Goch (Red Comb). This most serious undertaking requires special care and is not recommended in high winds and if done in winter it requires special skills, ice axe and crampons are a must.

<u>Crib Goch:</u>

The route starts from the car park at Pen-y-Pass, go through the gap in the wall at the upper right side of the car park and head westwards on a well marked path. This lower route is also known as the Pyg track which leads you up to the col at Bwlch Moch (Pass of the Pigs).

From here the main path heads straight on towards Snowdon, a right hand deviation takes you up the lower east ridge defended by the initial difficulties of the lower rock barrier. Be sure not to wander off too far to the left when approaching the rock wall which starts the scramble, this can lead to dangerous ground.

Sustained scrambling brings you to easier ground, the route is well marked and zigzags up the buttress on the crest of the ridge. In good conditions a competent scrambler will have no problems, though care should be taken as the ground is steep. Also, wet and greasy rocks can be a problem and the ridge should never be tackled in high winds.

The route is well marked so follow the obvious crest of the ridge to the secondary popular summit of Crib Goch 3,023 feet. Crib Goch and pinnacle ridge the jewel in the crown of the famous "Horseshoe" with excellent exposed scrambling on a knife edge ridge, it captures the very essence of the "coup de theatre" situation of wonderment.

From the popular summit, where the east ridge meets the north 3,023 ft, carefully proceed passing the table section of flat rock slab until the sharp knife edge, (no turning back now) It is possible to walk keeping upright balancing along the ridge, but it's best to play on the side of caution and keep three points of contact using the rock as a hand rail as you traverse across, try not to use your knees for this will cause problems, the vertical exposure you may find intimidating but the holds are all there to find.

Snowdon Horseshoe

Snowdon 3560 ft

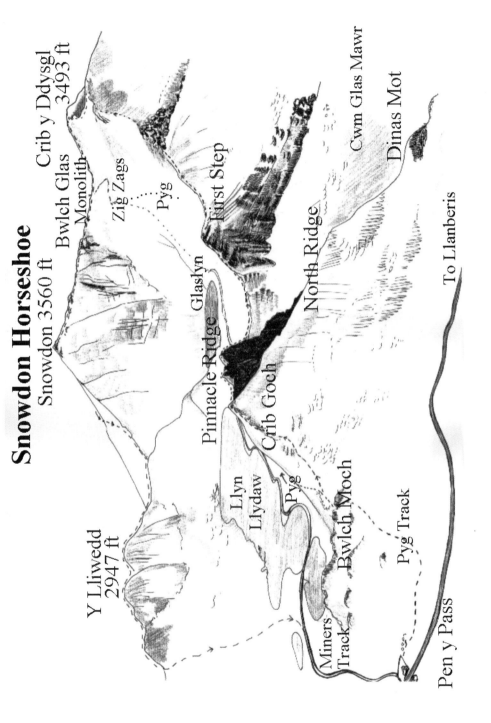

Crib y Ddysgl 3493 ft

Bwlch Glas

Monolith

Zig Zags

Pyg

First Step

Glaslyn

Cwm Glas Mawr

Dinas Mot

North Ridge

Pinnacle Ridge

Crib Goch

To Llanberis

Y Lliwedd 2947 ft

Llyn Llydaw

Pyg

Bwlch Moch

Pyg Track

Miners Track

Pen y Pass

THE SNOWDON HORSESHOE

The pinnacles are best climbed direct though steep, watch out for unreliable holds on the main ridge, for it is advisable to test all suspect holds as the burden of many feet can take it's toll especially at busy periods. The first and highest of the three pinnacles (the true summit 3,026 ft) is taken by directly passing a cairn of stones that marks the summit, between the first and second pinnacle gap a strenuous chock stone chimney slightly left brings you onto the second of the pinnacles.

Again the gap between the second and the third pinnacle is reached, taken slightly to the right use the series of exposed slanting ledges from left to right. A short scramble brings you onto the summit of the third pinnacle where a simple gully down climb and a scree path takes you to Bwlch Coch, where the first step of Crib y Ddysgl awaits you.

CRIB Y DDYSGL (The Second Section)

A short walk from Bwlch Coch brings you to a rock buttress which when climbed will bring you onto the ridge of Crib y Ddysgl, the route through the buttress, though steep, is well supplied with good holds and is well marked, the ridge itself is nowhere near as difficult and is best taken direct, though an easier path lies off to the right. After the main ridge there is one little final step which is short and easy, though steep, then the broader open walk to the trig pointed summit.

SNOWDON SUMMIT   (The Third Section)

Head south-west down the mountain to the rim of Bwlch Glas to where the great monolith stone protects the finish of the Pyg track. Follow a very good path which runs parallel to the rack and pinion railway line leading to the summit station, the main summit stands proud to the left of the station. To descend safely it is best to follow the path down the south-west ridge for some 200 metres to where a large marker stone divides the path to the left, the Watkin path takes you safely down to Bwlch y Saethau (Pass of the Arrows) to the fourth and final section of the route.

THE SNOWDON HORSESHOE

TRAVERSE OF LLIWEDD (The Fourth Section)

A straight forward scramble up the north-west ridge, the twin summits of Lliwedd are easily attained. Tremendous views all round, then a welcome descent following the ridge round to the north-east finally down to the shores of Llyn Llydaw, then turning right before the causeway onto the more wider Miners track to finish at Pen y Pass.

MOMMS TIPS

HYPOTHERMIA:

SYMPTOMS........... Shivering, Stumbling, Impaired speech or vision, Lethargy, Irrational behaviour and Gradual Unconsciousness then Death.

TREATMENT.......... Prevent further heat loss, Rest, Dry windproof clothing,
Keep head warm, Shelter from wind , Hot sweet drinks
No alcohol, Bodily warmth from others, Reassure patient
Hypothermia exhaustion is greatly accelerated by fear.

REMEMBER........... To place the patient with the head slightly lower than the body and if evacuation is required place the patient on the stretcher and transport with the head facing down hill.

REMEMBER THAT IF A MEMBER OF YOUR PARTY GOES DOWN WITH HYPOTHERMIA THEN OTHER MEMBERS INCLUDING YOURSELF MAYBE DANGEROUSLY CLOSE TO HYPOTHERMIA.

A technical climb of 300 feet
climb the rock face and don't be beat,
If you abseil down to descend
use figure of eight it will be your friend.

TECHNICAL ABILITY

To assure an all round basic technical mountaineering ability certain skills with the rope and basic rock work are required. A rock climb of at least 300 feet on a graded route of your personal choice, either leader or second with full safety use of the rope with the understanding of belays and protection, with the use of a selection of rope knots and the ability to abseil in an emergency.

To abseil is to descend rapidly in a controlled manner by sliding down a rope either in the true classic style, semi classic style or by using a friction device called a Figure of Eight Descender. *(Fig No 11)*

Care should be taken when abseiling, for the technique is at best hazardous! Common causes of accidents while abseiling are the loss of control, anchor or belay failure, jamming of the friction device by loose fittings or hair. Abseiling off the end of the rope can catch out the unwary, as well as stone fall caused by abseiling off over loose rocks.

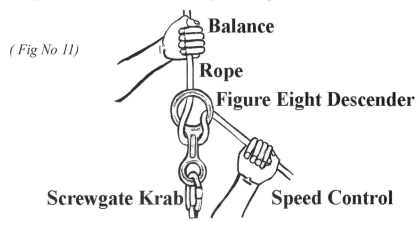

(Fig No 11) **Balance**

Rope

Figure Eight Descender

Screwgate Krab **Speed Control**

The Momms recommend using the Figure of Eight descender, a friction device made of alloy rings joined together like a numerical eight, the smaller ring attaches to the climbing harness using a screw gate karabiner while the rope runs through and around the larger ring, the descent is controlled by varying the angle of the lower rope.

*On Pen Yr Ole Wen's great face of Braich ty du
climb the Pinnacle for all to see.*

THE BRAICH TY DU PINNACLE

Follow the A5 road out of Bethesda towards the beautiful valley of Ogwen, to the left lies the simmering lake of Llyn Ogwen nesting below the slopes of Pen yr Ole Wen towering some 3,210 feet above.

From the Ogwen cottages G.R. 649604 where the start of the normal route up Pen yr Ole Wen zigzags its way up the south ridge, here lies the key to the west face or better known Braich ty du face. Walk down the road some 300 yards towards Bethesda, to the right look upwards and on the lower ribbed arete stands the distinctive twin pinnacles of your Momms quest.

Now it is easy to climb up and over the wall and head straight upwards, but! the lower slopes consist of unstable scree and rocks which can be easily dislodged onto the road below.

So having viewed and pinpointed the pinnacles head back towards the Ogwen cottages, cross the road to the left where the stile joins the main path on the north side of the road bridge, follow the main south ridge path for some 25 metres then contour left passing below rocky buttresses on an ill-defined path, care should be taken when traversing the lower slopes because of the unstable scree.

When the narrow pinnacle ridge is reached keep to the right hand couloir and climb up to a broken wall that runs from left to right, cross the wall and follow the grassy slope upwards to the left, an exposed grassy ramp comes into view, edge round to the right turning the corner (take care and use a rope if wet) to find a short staircase of rock blocks leading upwards onto the ridge. The edge of which leads to a ledge below a ten foot step, the step taken slightly on the right using large hand holds, the exposed pinnacles are ahead and at your finger tips. Good luck! Now retrace your route safely down.

Pinnacles

The Ledge

Staircase
Blocks

Corner

Grass Ramp

Grass
Slope

Wall

Scree
Slope

Route

Dangerous Screes Below

MOMMS TIPS

Italian Friction Hitch

A knot for a single rope, useful for bringing up a second on a direct or indirect belay, it can also be used in place of a figure of Eight Descender for an abseil with a screwgate karabiner in an emergency, this knot has the great advantage of utilising basic equipment.

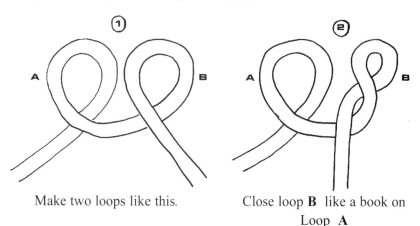

Make two loops like this.   Close loop **B** like a book on
                                            Loop **A**

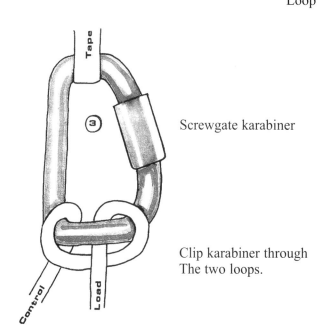

Screwgate karabiner

Clip karabiner through
The two loops.

WELL DONE

Then finally make your way down
to the boozer in the nearby town.

A celebratory drink is on the agenda
call at the Vic in nearby Bethesda.

All I would like to say at this stage is, well done! All the feats of the Momms completed, now it's time to reflect on what you've achieved and how far you've come in mountaineering terms. Which of course is best done propping up the bar where the Momms poem was born, "in the Victoria Hotel" on the high street in Bethesda, successfully washed down with your celebratory pint, followed by any other pub that can be found in this friendly and hard working Welsh town.

THE CURSE OF THE MOMMS

And reflect on those who've lied
The curse of the Momms will decide
Of what fate that will become
The liar, the cheat, the spineless one.

The Momms challenge is somewhat unusual in that apart from the feats involved there are no written rules on how and when to complete them, this narrows the challenge to a more personal level.

So that to cheat is to cheat oneself, the Momms is done by you for you and only you know the inner truth. You cannot lie to yourself and this is where the last verse comes in, so don't forget the curse of the Momms.........!

By accident verbal reference was made to the red bandanna scarf worn by myself as a Momms scarf, this I've adopted so the words " To earn the badge just come along, endure the challenge of the Mom" also refers to the much sought after red bandanna and the badge that indicates the Momms feats.

Momms certificates are also available with each Mom being registered and given a registration number that's entered into the "Book of Momms" and currently shown on the Momms Website............ Momms.net

For a current price list of Momms certification and registration, badges and bandanna scarfs etc send S.A.E. to,

Momms Challenge
T. Atkinson
28 Sheridan Street,
Outwood,
Wakefield,
West Yorkshire.
WF1 3TP

MOMMS TIPS

HOW TO SAVE A LIFE

I don't want to try to drill first aid into every potential would be Mom but I'd like to mention just one thing that could make the difference between life and death and that is the A.B.C. Rule.

AIRWAY   BREATHING   CIRCULATION

AIRWAY:

Just by opening someone's Airway can save a life.

If breathing has stopped, and the casualty cannot be aroused and looks truly comatose (blue lips) then kneel beside the casualty and lift the chin forwards with the index and middle finger of one hand while pressing the forehead backwards with the heel of the other hand.

This will extend the head and the neck and lift the tongue forwards clearing the airway, if the casualty is capable of breathing this will trigger a response, you can then place them in the recovery position. *(Fig No 12)*

BREATHING:

If there is no response having ensured a good airway then keep the head tilted back and begin mouth to mouth breathing, open your mouth wide and take a deep breath, pinch the casualty by the nostrils with your fingers, seal your lips round their mouth and blow into their lungs watching for their chest to rise and fall.   Determine whether the casualty's heart is beating by checking the carotid pulse which is found by placing two fingers on the Adams apple and moving them to the side into the groove between the cartilage and the prominent muscle that runs from the base of the ear.

If breathing returns and there's a pulse turn the casualty into the recovery position.

HOW TO SAVE A LIFE

CIRCULATION:

If there's no response having checked for a pulse start cardiac massage, kneel by the casualty, by the left side with your hands crossed together, place them on the lower breast bone and lean forward sharply onto straight arms pressing down on to the heel of the hand ten times. Then inflate the lungs again with two breaths then repeat the process, hopefully having revived the casualty, examine the body "head to toe" for bleeding and broken bones.

Excessive bleeding can be stopped by direct pressure with the hand or pad and elevation of the injured limb.

Broken bones, signs..... Pain, Swelling and Deformity, Immobilise to prevent shock and further damage but don't attempt to straighten limbs. If the casualty is conscious and complains of back pain and numbness don't attempt to move them until the neck and back are held immobile, this is best done by the Mountain Rescue Team.

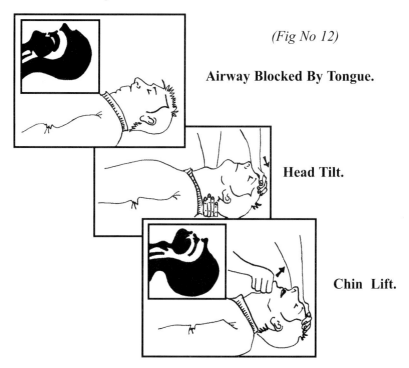

(Fig No 12)

Airway Blocked By Tongue.

Head Tilt.

Chin Lift.

62

MOMMS CHECK LIST

The Feats	Comments	Tick Box
Shutlingsloe		
Ben Nevis		
Snowdon		
Scafell Pike		
Yorkshire 3 Peaks		
Pen y Ghent		
Whernside		
Ingleborough		
12,000 Foot Peak		
Welsh XIV		
Jack's Rake		
North Ridge Tryfan		
Adam & Eve Jump		
Bristly Ridge		
Snowdon Horseshoe		
Crib Goch		
Crib y Ddysgl		
Snowdon		
Y Lliwedd		
300 Foot Rock Climb		
Belay & Abseiling		
Castell y Gwynt		
Braich ty du Pinnacle		
Pint in the Victoria Hotel		

I the undersigned do claim membership of the Momms

Signature..Date..

Printed Name..

Address..

Momms certificate and registration current price list S.A.E.
to Momms Challenge,
T. Atkinson, 28 Sheridan Street, Outwood, Wakefield, West Yorkshire WF1 3TP

MOUNTAINEERING POEMS

Really Bold

Mountaineers are very strong
The sweat they make must really Pong!
They Climb higher and higher in the sky
Whilst the snow is slowly passing by,
They get ever so cold
Climbing mountains really bold

By Nicola Soanes & Amy C. Atkinson - Age 9

In the Mountains

In the mountains you get snowy weather
So I think mountaineers are very clever,
I think this because they don't slip about
Well the gear saves them from slipping out.

By Nicola Soanes - Age 9

My Dad & his Mountains

My dad is mad
But he's never sad,
He climbs many mountains high
They go right to the sky.
He never gives in
He's in the world to win
I've climbed some with him
And he never gave in.

By Amy C. Atkinson - Age 9

ACCOMMODATION:

Ben Nevis Area:

Campsites:

Glen Nevis Caravan & Camping Park 01397 702191
Lochy Caravan & Camping 01397 703446

Youth Hostels & Bunkhouses

Fort William Backpackers 01397 700711
Glen Nevis Youth Hostel 01397 702336
Ben Nevis Bunkhouse
Achintee Farm 01397 702240

Bed & Breakfast

Glenlochy Guest House 01397 702909
Rhu Mhor Guest House 01397 702213

Scafell Area:

Wasdale Head Camping 019467 26220
Wasdale Head Hall Youth Hostel 019467 26222
Wasdale Head Inn 019467 26229

Pavey Ark Langdale:

Old Dungeon Ghyll Hotel 015394 37272
New Dungeon Ghyll Hotel 015394 37213
Camping Great Langdale 015394 37668
B&B   Lacet House, Ambleside 015394 34342

Three Peaks Area:

Camping Holme Farm 01729 860281
The Crown Hotel, Horton in Ribblesdale 01729 860209
Golden Lion Hotel, Horton in Ribblesdale 01729 860206
Pen y ghent cafe, Horton in Ribblesdale 01729 860333

65

Bethesda & Snowdon Area:

Campsites/Bed & Breakfast:

Dolgam, Capel Curig...01690 720228
Hafod Lydan, Llanberis..01286 870356
Snowdon House, Nant Peris...01286 870718
Pen y Pass Youth Hostel..01286 870428
B&B Victoria Hotel, Bethesda 01248 600481
Marteg, Llanberis..01286 870207
Plas Coch, Llanberis 01286 872122
Bron y Graig, Llanberis..01286 872073

Chamonix Mont Blanc:

Office du Tourisme..0033 4 50 53 00 24

NOTES

Check out the Momms Web Site:
Http//www.momms.net

Challenge Publications
Http//www.chall-pub.fsnet.co.uk